Making This Life Work

Living Your Best Life

By: Dr. Chris Hubbard Jackson

Publisher: Miller Christenson Group LLC
11001 Dunklin Drive #38611, St. Louis, MO 63138
www.millerchristensongroup.com
millerchristensongroupllc@gmail.com

Author Information & Speaking Engagements
Dr. Chris Hubbard Jackson
Facebook: Dr Chris HJ
Instagram: drchris_hj
Twitter: DrChris_HJ

This book is *not* intended as a substitute for medical or psychological advice. The reader should regularly consult a physician in matters relating to her/his health and particularly with respect to any symptoms that may require diagnosis or medical attention.

ISBN-13:   978-1-951586-00-3
eBook ISBN-13:   978-1-951586-01-0

Dedication

This book is dedicated to women everywhere who feel burdened by their blessings. To women who suffer in silence while trying to have it all. Take your Superwoman cape off girl.

Thank you to the women in my tribe for all that you are and all that you do. A special thank you to Ella, Tiffany B., Grandma Hubbard, Aunt Carolyn, and many others. You are appreciated more than you know.

A final thanks to Melissa King, gone but never forgotten. You are truly loved and missed.

Enjoy the life you chose. – Author Unknown

Table of Contents

Introduction

Welcome to success, for some the hallmark of a good life. I'd bought into the whole you can have it all mantra. You know the one about having the perfect kids, perfect neighborhood, perfect job, perfect husband, and perfect body. I was working hard to be perfect and to balance my life. I was mastering it pretty well too — or so I thought.

About six months after the birth of my second child, I woke up one day to find myself miserable, angry, hopeless, and empty. I was puzzled by my circumstances and wondered how I got there. I cried and cried hard. I talked to friends, close loved ones, and my husband. I wanted to be sure this wasn't postpartum depression, and it wasn't. This life was supposed to be my happily ever after and I wasn't happy. Cue the halos and opera music, but all I heard was silence. Dead silence.

1

I had previously been a single parent of teens (not biologically mine), gotten married, had a baby, and gotten divorced. After the teens graduated and moved out, I struggled a few years trying to parent a toddler, get my career together, finish my education, and start a new life. I thought my second marriage would be a fresh start and would fix ALL the disappointment that had plagued my life. Oh, how wrong I was.

From the outside looking in, my life was perfect. I had a good husband, good job, nice home, nice cars, beautiful children, degrees, great friends, good health, and my prayer life was in order. Even my husband didn't understand why I wasn't happy. I'm sure you are probably thinking you'd trade places with me in a heartbeat, and I'm being a spoiled ungrateful princess. Before you judge me, hear me out.

With ALL these wonderful things came a LOT of added responsibility and I felt like I was drowning. The cost of the oil in my alabaster box was too high and I was ready to burn it or walk away. None of this made sense for those who didn't know the intimate details of my life.

Let me explain. Getting a divorce rocked me to my core so I had made some promises to myself which I hadn't done a good job of keeping. Since I wasn't true to myself, I found myself struggling and suffering. I felt alone, distant, and afraid. I talked, prayed, and wept until there were no tears left. Then I became angry because anger is what I knew I could count on when I had nothing to give.

Anger was my foundation. It cradled me, took care of me, and was always there faithfully when needed. It got me up and moving. Quite frankly, my anger got stuff done when I didn't know how I was going to do it. Anger was my ride or die and had been with me since childhood. Anger was my provider, strength, energy, and driving force on those days when I had NOTHING left. Plus being vulnerable wasn't an option, so any feeling of weakness had to be replaced with a different feeling that strengthened me. Anger empowered me and had become my not so invisible cloak.

This season in my life was different. This time anger was destroying me. No matter how I yelled and screamed, and spewed my venom, I didn't feel the same release I had felt in the past. It wasn't working and I had to find a new way of functioning if I planned to survive and thrive. Maybe you can relate to my story. For you anger may be your security blanket or maybe food or playing the victim or blaming or working too much or something else. Whatever *it* is probably isn't working anymore so let's figure out how to make this life work.

I was supposed to be living the dream, but in reality I was exhausted, tired, and resentful. Heck I was doing too much in the hopes of having a perfect life. I'm sure you can relate all too well. Like me, you probably thought "I can be a successful career woman with well-behaved kids, an immaculate house, handsome husband, and have a banging body. I got this!" Yeah, and like me you've probably figured out having it all just might cost you your sanity and possibly your edges. No ma'am I'm not here for that and neither are you. Neither are you!

The whole going to work, raising kids, tending the house, cleaning, cooking, grocery shopping, attending parent teacher association (PTA) meetings, homework, sleep overs, praying faithfully, spending time with friends, and swinging from the chandelier for bae, is too much AND! Unless you are going to clone yourself or cut yourself in half or hire a team or get a couple sister wives, something must change.

It's time to come to terms with the life you have chosen and figure out how to make it work. I mean really work for you so that you can live YOUR best life. Not the life others had in mind for you, but the one YOU CHOSE for yourself. You must be okay for you. Who are you trying to impress with your life? Do you really need to do *all* those things? What exactly are you trying to do? You can have it all, but you can't DO it all by yourself.

This book is intended to be a great tool for women, especially moms who are stressed out, burdened, overwhelmed, or fed-up with the AND in their lives. In the chapters that follow are the steps that I took to get me to where I needed to be. A healthier, happier, more fulfilled, less stressed version of myself was who I wanted to be. The order of them was my journey. The chapters can be read alone or in the sequence that works for you, but read them all. Each chapter has valuable insight which will help you to transition. But when you're ready and ONLY when YOU ARE ready.

This journey is going to take work, and the end result is totally up to you. It'll stretch you as far as you are willing to work to grow. The world and everyone in it are merely spectators on your journey. You are in total control. Only you can save you!

Some chapters of this book are revelation, some are clarification, and some are confirmation. Revelation, clarification, and confirmation may vary depending on the topic. Only you will know what this book will do for you. Different seasons may cause you to reference different chapters. Read, reflect, and renew.

Please note, this book is real and straight forward. I'm the friend who says what everyone is thinking but is afraid to say. I don't handle people with kid gloves. I believe in tactful tough love with a side of humor. Throughout this book I use colorful yet classy language with a bit of edge. My intent isn't to offend you or to come for your head, but rather to lovingly snatch you off the proverbial ledge. So, catch the vibe girl, there's more room to learn and laugh in my tribe.

As you may have noticed by my mention of prayer, this book has religious references and scriptures. However, the general principles are still useful for Christians and non-Christians. So, don't get distracted by the scripture, but instead connect with the concepts. I'm not trying to convert you.

I just know that other women are facing the same struggles that I am. They say women don't like women and don't get along very well, but I'm not one of those women. So, when I figured out a way to make my life work so I could live my best life, I thought I would share. Going through this journey made me feel free again, and I found me again. Will you join me?

Preparation for the Journey

Like me, I'm guessing life isn't quite meeting your needs. Let's do some prep work to figure out how to make your life work. Make a list of the top 5 things that if these things worked, your life would improve drastically. Then make a list of the 5 things in your life which are working well. Then list whatever challenges you have. Use additional paper or an app on your phone, if needed. You may also fill in all of the answers via either link

http://bit.ly/MTLWsurvey

https://forms.gle/9LPP3ByxfWRG41Ns9

What needs work?

1. _____

2. _____

3. _____

4. _____

5. _____

What's working well?

1. _____

2. _____

3. _____

4. _____

5. _____

What are the challenges?

1. _____

2. _____

3. _____

4. _____

5. _____

Of your top 5 things that need work, pick the 3 which are most important and label them A (most important), B (second most important), C (third most important). Great start! Now, which of the things that work well, can assist you in making your top 3 work? Which of the challenges impact your top 3? As you read this book keep your top 3 in mind. However, don't get stuck on them. You may find some solutions for some items. You may also find that some things become less important the further you read along and reprioritize your life. We'll see as we journey into making this life work so you can live your best life.

Chapter 1:
No More Superwoman

You can have it all, but you can't DO it all by yourself. -- Dr. Chris Hubbard Jackson

Stop Overfunctioning, Perfectionism, and People Pleasing

I was the chronic overfunctioner. Yes, the person who did things for people that they could do for themselves. I was the person who helped everyone pull their load. I was considerate and I babied people in the name of love. What I was really doing was stealing opportunities for others to be more independent.

Take for example a baby who grows into a toddler. At first the baby needs your help all the time. As the baby grows into a toddler, he becomes more self-sufficient and you start to hear things like "I can do that myself." If you allow him to do things, the toddler will show pride in his work and will show off his new skills. However, if you keep doing things for him, the toddler will either battle you by resisting your help or he'll just give in and you'll do it ALL. You'll look up one day and your pudgy little toddler will be a bossy four-year old who can't tie his shoes and insists on riding in a stroller even though he's way too big.

If you find that you must be needed, then you may have developed some codependency. Codependency is when you have "dependence on the needs of or control by another" (Merriam-Webster.com). That codependent toddler eventually grows up to be a codependent man-child who lacks the ability to function in a normal relationship. I've dated a man-child or two and I'm sure you have too, so you know what I'm talking about.

With those I cherished the most, I was codependent in the name of love. I needed

14

them to need me but complained about being needed. Right. Read that again. No really! Are you tired of helping people, but feel like you must help? Are you the one that takes care of things? Like in case of emergency call [insert your name here].

Take a moment to think, really think. Be honest with yourself. If the answer is "yes" then you my friend may be codependent. You get no judgment from me, but if you want your freedom back, let's fix it. If you always do it for them, they will never do it for themselves. Don't cripple them with codependency. Codependency is not love.

In helping others, I wore my Superwoman cape proudly with all its rips and stains. But... the burden of helping EVERYONE else was too much. I gave and gave and gave, but it was never enough. All they did was take, take, take, and I became dust bowl dry and bitter. I helped and complained and helped and complained. I was a busy body, a meddler, a know it all, and I was forever helping. When I wasn't helping others, I was focused on ensuring that what was done for me was done to perfection. I mean, why do something unless you're going to do it right? I helped other people, but truthfully, I didn't know how to accept help. Does that last part sound familiar?

I called it independence, but in reality I was a perfectionist who had some control issues. I believed if it was to be done right, I'd probably be better off doing it myself. I'd ask people to do things and if they didn't do them when I felt I wanted or needed them to be done, then I'd do them myself. Or, maybe it's just me, but I get the sense you've been doing some of this too.

If I asked someone (excluding children) to do something and it didn't get done when I wanted or when they agreed to do it, then I didn't ask again. People learned this quickly about me and used it to their full advantage.

They'd wait me out and they are waiting you out too.

Face it girl, I'm doing too much, you are doing too much, and the AND is too much. My cape was raggedy and putting it on was exhausting so after a few years, I stopped everything. I went on strike and for two and a half months my answer was "no, you take care of it." I guess they figured waiting me out would work and I'd fix things, but I was fed-up, so I didn't do anything. I told them what needed to be done, and that I wasn't going to do it anymore. Some things got done and some things didn't.

It was painful to not do things, but it was necessary. I truly didn't have any energy to give so I gave myself all that I had. I know you are thinking "I can't do that." "If I do that things will fail or fall apart." "That's just not how I do things!" Okay, but if you keep doing it all, THEY NEVER WILL! That's kids, family, co-workers, friends, mates. Nobody, yes

17

NOBODY will feel the need or desire to help or to do for themselves. So, sit down Superwoman. No More!

The great thing about my break was that no one was injured, things didn't fall apart, and we weren't living in squalor. They adjusted and stopped using me as their default. I freed their dependence on me and loved them more because of it. Now they didn't like the change and quite frankly acted like babies, throwing tantrums and being overly dramatic, but they survived. All attempts to make me feel bad were quickly rebuked because they could do so much more themselves and I was going to **let them**. You should let them too.

Who in your life could do more for themselves if you showed them?

_____

_____

What minor non-life threatening or career ending tasks can you put down or transfer over to others?

_____

_____

What is keeping your Superwoman cape on? No really, why won't you let go?

_____

_____

Take a moment to regroup and breathe. From this experience you'll learn that some things will get done but many things won't. You'll need to be okay with that. I found out that things were super important and had to get done, when I was doing them for people. However, when they had to do them, they didn't do them because they said they weren't that important. That was fine by me. You'll see the same sort of thing too.

Mind you, when it comes to kids, you'll have to insist on some things getting done such as baths, laundry, cleaning their rooms, or whatever the mandatory chores of your house are. Otherwise they won't do them, and they won't be bothered. You'll also have to learn to be unbothered by things that don't get done that are not critical or necessary. If it doesn't impact you or your household or job (or whatever else you hold dear) in a major life altering way, turn a blind eye. Say nothing when they don't do it. Resist the urge to fuss. No more Superwoman, no more!

You can't stay on strike forever, so you'll have to figure out how to make this life work. Focus on doing the critical things and let others deal with the rest. Anything others can do for themselves; you should stop doing. Provide suggestions on how they can get things done efficiently. For example, any child age six or older who can work a smart phone or Blu-ray player, can do laundry. I'm talking about

sorting, washing, drying, and putting it away.
If you Google "age appropriate chores" you'll
find plenty of websites, such as this WebMD
article.

https://www.webmd.com/parenting/features/chores-for-children#1

What things can you stop doing today?

_____

_____

What things can you train others to do at home?

_____

_____

What things can you train others to do at work?

_____

_____

Boundaries: The Keys to Freedom

Taking off the Superwoman cape was the first part, now let's stay free. Boundaries are the key part of not overfunctioning and people pleasing. When I was going through my mind trying to figure out what could be done, I also started to think about how things got that way. It was because I didn't use "NO" enough and I was too accommodating. I didn't have proper boundaries. In setting boundaries you'll have to re-establish what is okay and to what degree, or what is not okay, in how people treat you.

It is NOT okay to sacrifice YOUR time or YOUR needs or feelings **constantly**. That is not necessary, in order to love others. You see society tricks you into believing that in order to be a good person, wife, mother, or another role you have, then you must give and be selfless. The problem with this thinking is that many times you run yourself in the ground trying to prove how selfless you are.

Your value isn't gauged by your suffering and neither is your love. I've seen immaculate homes become filthy hoarding prisons because people pushed and demanded until someone broke. Then they sit back and talk bad about you because they don't see why you're acting like this. Mind you their judgment never comes with an offer of assistance or true consideration of your feelings.

If you're tempted to hold on to your cape for a little while longer, just remember, your Superwoman cape won't protect you from hurt feelings. Keeping the cape on or putting it back on will leave you hurt and tired, because now you know better. Know there is a better way to make your life work, that doesn't include exhausting yourself.

Do you feel the pressure to put others' needs above your own?

A lot   Some   Not At All

How much do you feel the need to prove how self-less you are?

A lot   Some   Not At All

How much of your time is being spent on other people?

A lot   Some   Not At All

Here are some questions to ask yourself in order to establish healthy boundaries.

How much access do you allow people?

A lot   Some   Not At All

What parts of you do you want people to have access to? For instance, emotions, finances, time, mental energy, etc.

_____

_____

How much access do you want people to have?

A lot   Some   Not At All

Are there rules or reasons that certain people have more access than others? Why?

_____

_____

Boundaries are healthy and necessary. You are a person, *not* a possession. You don't have to allow people access to **all** of you. Learn to say "NO" and mean it. Then don't feel guilty about it. Some people will try to manipulate you into feeling guilty because when you say "NO," they get less. Why would they want less of a resource as great as you? Yes, I said resource. Your time, energy, money, and willingness to help, are **all** viewed as a resource and precious commodity. Be wise by saying "NO."

Now don't say "NO" to everything or become obnoxiously selfish. What I'm saying is to guard your heart, time, and mind, without being bitter, mean, angry, rude, arrogant, hurt, or guilty. Ensure you are not sacrificing what you need, in order to meet *other* people's needs. This applies wholeheartedly to dealing with adults, but for underage children some sacrifices may be needed. Even then, these sacrifices shouldn't be all the time. If you have limited resources, I've been there too, and we'll tackle that in the chapters to come.

Saying "NO" will give you hours in the day back. So, come down off their pedestal and strip away that heavy cape of perfection that's crushing you. The world doesn't own you and you don't owe anyone anything. Your responsibilities are NOT indebtedness. I repeat... your responsibilities are not a debt you owe!

If people's love and kindness are contingent upon what you do for them, or how you meet their needs, or how much you sacrifice to get things done, then that's not genuine and you'll never be enough. A title isn't ownership when it comes to people. Your mom, aunt, sister, grandmother, or other relatives don't own you.

Reclaim your life by putting proper boundaries in place. Start by determining what's healthy to give and give it. Expect that there will be some moments of legitimate exceptions and adjust accordingly, but beware of sliding back into the people pleasing or perfectionism trap. You are too important to be used.

Some people will use you if you let them. Some people will also try to use your insecurities in order to manipulate you into doing something for them. For example, if your mom was an alcoholic who neglected her mate and kids, people may attempt to manipulate you by saying you're not a good mom if you don't…. You're not a good sister if you don't… You're not a good daughter if you don't… They will form whatever story is needed to push you into giving in to their demands.

I know it's terrible, but some people will try you. The people you love most are usually the ones who feel most entitled to the pieces of you. Many without regard to how that access makes you feel. For some people if your glass is half full, they can use it to top themselves off. Boundaries are the key and any relationship without proper boundaries is a recipe for disaster.

Who are your constant boundary breakers?

_____

_____

How can you reset the relationship and get the constant boundary breakers back in line?

_____

_____

Emotional Boundaries: The Deadbolt Key to Freedom

While you are setting boundaries, don't forget about the emotional ones. Restrict access to your emotions. Now I don't mean you should disconnect or shutdown emotionally. What I'm saying is that not every situation or person should have the same amount of access to your emotional space. When you allow too much in, you become bogged down, overwhelmed, frustrated, angry, depressed, and depleted.

In restricting emotional access, you must ask yourself the following:
1. Is an emotional response necessary?
2. Will an emotional response help this situation?
3. What good will I gain from connecting to this emotionally?

Take a step back and objectively consider those three questions about every person and situation who is impacting your life. Now respond appropriately. By limiting access to your emotions, you decrease the likelihood of emotional exhaustion. According to healthline.com, emotional exhaustion is "a state of feeling emotionally worn-out and drained as a result of accumulated stress from your personal or work lives, or a combination of both.

Some factors that contribute to emotional exhaustion are:

1. Having a baby or raising children
2. Financial stress
3. High pressure jobs or working long hours
4. Going through a prolonged divorce
5. Pursuing your education
6. Living with a chronic illness or injury
7. Caring for a loved one or caring for a loved one with a chronic illness or injury

8. Relationship problems or relationship instability

9. Work-life conflict

10. Poor person-job fit

https://www.healthline.com/health/emotional-exhaustion#causes

Now, how many of the factors on the list sound like your life? I bet like me; you've selected quite a few. No wonder you're feeling overwhelmed. If thinking about all the AND in your life has left you a bit uneasy, take a moment to gather yourself.

Breathe deeply and fight the urge to allow it to take root. If it has already taken root, then breathe it out. Inhale and count to five in your head. I mean really inhale deeply and think about all that is bogging you down emotionally. Decide to either hold on to it or let it go. Exhale from your gut and let it all go. Pull your stomach in as you push the emotions out. Repeat if you didn't get it all the first time.

Once you let it all go, then be determined not to let it come back. Take care of yourself. Do yoga or work out or practice mindful meditation. Try joining a small group at church or another group that focuses on something you are interested in. The goal here is to find a healthy release and time to yourself.

If you feel like you need just a bit more, then consider some counseling or coaching. If you have a job with insurance benefits, usually there is an Employee Assistance Program (EAP) that you can access about five sessions for no charge. If you have Medicaid or medical coverage, assistance is there. Check the website or call the customer service number on the back of the card. The sessions are confidential.

Maybe you don't want to talk about your childhood or trauma, but you just need to vent in a protected space and learn some tips for moving forward. A counselor could help with that. Now if you think counselors are for crazy people, hear me out. You can become "crazy" when you harbor your emotions instead of dealing with them in a healthy way. Or maybe you just ignore your issues away. Speaking from experience, you can only ignore yourself and your issues for so long before they begin to leak out. Before you know it, you'll be an unpredictable emotional mess, and not know why. Don't ignore yourself.

Do you get the feeling that something is wrong, but you don't know why?

A lot   Some   Not At All

Do you often feel tired, but don't know why?

A lot   Some   Not At All

Do you go to bed tired and wake up tired?

A lot   Some   Not At All

What is keeping you from talking to someone? For example, finances, embarrassment, lack of trust in people, don't know where to find someone, or something else.

_____

_____

Take Care of Yourself

I forgot to take care of myself and it wasn't until I was filled with resentment that I realized I was pouring from an empty cup. I was depleted, spiritually dry, and fed up. The odd thing is I couldn't put my finger on why. I watched the "Surviving Loss" episode of Jada Pinkett-Smith's Red Table Talk, and I was finally able to give my emotional state a name. I'd lost myself and it didn't happen all at once. I was fighting for my life to maintain who I was. How do you know you've lost yourself you ask? Oh, you'll realize it when you keep having that empty, uneasy feeling with a side of hopelessness. That feeling of something being wrong, but you don't know why.

My life was changing, and it required me to give more of myself than I had to give. I had mastered being a single parent and I was okay in that state but wanted more. Then I was okay with a husband and a self-sufficient child. I was able to volunteer, serve on boards, serve at our daughter's school, help him, tend to our house, and still have time for myself. A new child, especially a new baby meant I'd have to come out of my comfort zone and figure out a new way of being. I was going to have to figure out how to make this life work.

Changes in your family structure or lifestyle such as this, or just within a short amount of time, will impact you. You may start to feel like you've lost time for yourself and eventually you may feel as if you've completely lost yourself. If you're feeling this way, it's because you aren't taking care of yourself.

35

You're probably putting everyone else's needs before your own and you are suffocating. I know I gave and gave, leaving nothing for myself. Not taking care of yourself will have you dying on the inside while fighting on the outside. You'll go to bed tired and wake up tired because you aren't taking care of yourself. You may also be miserable!

I walked myself through my emotions and I also had to deal with my truths. Even in all that, I still wasn't okay. I'd lost myself and needed to get myself back. But how?!? Thankfully I was fortunate enough to take a 5-day vacation alone. During my 5-day retreat I prayed and processed my emotions. I really figured out why I was feeling how I was feeling and made a commitment to myself to be more emotionally healthy. I also accepted that the me I was, could no longer be. She was no longer equipped for the life I had, and I had to grow. That growth meant making time for myself and working on a new me. I came back from my vacation happy, rested, and restored. The happiest I'd been in years.

I know what you're thinking. That sounds great, but my life isn't setup for that. Mine wasn't always either. So, here's what you can do. I did it and still do it. I start each morning with 15-25 minutes of quiet time. I pray, praise, and meditate. If mornings aren't for you, try evenings or during your lunch. I get up early to make sure that I have that time alone. I go into the bathroom and I look at the Bible scripture on my phone, then I go into prayer. If another scripture is placed upon my heart, I read it. If I have concerns, I pray and meditate. If I'm struggling with something, I give it over to God.

In addition to taking time alone in the morning, I take one hour each week to reflect and journal my experiences. If you say you don't have an hour, maybe you don't have it all at once. Maybe you have it in 15-minute increments. You say, "Chris there are too many people in my house, and I have too much to do." Okay, so start where you are. What can you do to find a bit of peace and quiet?

After getting divorced I lived in a one-bedroom apartment with a teenager and a toddler. That didn't leave much alone time or quiet, so I had to make some. There were rules in the house that ensured that when I got off work I had at least 30 minutes to myself. Some days I had to take that 30 minutes sitting alone in my car in front of my apartment. On the days when the teen wasn't there, Elmo and Sesame Street were my best friends. A 30-minute episode with my earbuds in, did wonders for my mind.

On the days when I just wanted to get away, but couldn't really afford to, I'd put gas in my car and drive. I found places to drive within an hour or two away and I'd go there. The drive cleared my mind, and it caused the kids to sleep. I'd drive and listen to music.

We'd get there and sometimes just go to the park and eat lunches I'd packed. If there were free things to do, we'd do them.

You must take time to recharge yourself. You are worth it so make some time! I know you are, but do you think you are? You are worth at least an hour each week to yourself to get your head together and to renew. You must restore you each week or you'll wear yourself out. You are the most important person in your life, and YOU must care for you.

If you are fortunate enough to have time away or take a day off work or have a long weekend, then do it. Something else you can do is reach out to friends and family to see who will let you spend the night at their house. Explain to them that you need some time alone to rest and think. When selecting someone's house to go over, don't go over someone's house who has a lot of distractions or noise. The point is to relax and think, not find someone else to help. So if possible, get your kids situated and go. Going to someone else's house will ensure that you don't get distracted by household chores, and it may help you to relax. While you're there ask yourself the following questions.

Are you where you want to be in life?

Yes   No   Working on it

What can you do more of in order to feel better about your life?

_____

_____

Are you happy?

Yes   No   Working on it

What makes you happy?

_____

_____

_____

_____

_____

If you can't name five things that make you happy, then you have work to do. Before my journey I couldn't name anything. Now I can honestly say I love to watch the sun rise, because it's a reminder that God is still there and hears my prayers. I like to dance, even though I don't know the latest dance moves. I like fresh seafood. I love fruit dipped in dark chocolate. Most of all, I love time alone.

Your happiness is your responsibility and doesn't occur by chance. You must work for it. No one else can make you happy, but they can do or stop doing things that make you less miserable. Figure out what makes you happy and be happy. Take ownership for your happiness and well-being then take care of it.

How happy do you really want to be?

A lot   Some   Not At All

What does happiness look like for you?

_____

_____

Now I'm sure you've heard it a thousand times and even as you roll your eyes and say, "yeah I know," you have yet to do this critical thing for yourself. Everyone needs your help, but no one needs your help more than you. Even just 10 minutes of uninterrupted time to yourself each day, doing whatever you choose, can recharge and restore you. Show up for yourself. You must ensure you are giving yourself what YOU need. Face the facts, no one is coming to save you so save yourself. Making this life work starts with you. Yes ma'am, YOU. You are in charge of your world. Are you ready to live your best life?

Tips for putting down your Superwoman Cape:
1. Stop overfunctioning
2. Establish and maintain proper boundaries
3. Stop people pleasing
4. Make yourself a high priority

Chapter 2:
Let Go Then Get A Grip

"A cheerful heart is good medicine, but a broken spirit saps a person's strength."
Proverbs 17:22 NLT

Expectations...Just Say No

Frustration was a constant in my life because I couldn't understand why people were the way they were. I remember just sitting one day and going through my list of frustrations. You know the list. The one with plenty of people related problems that create other problems. I was chest deep in reviewing the list when I said to myself "STOP! Just STOP! How long are you going to be frustrated by this? You are tail chasing the same frustrations from last year and the year before. When are you going to get over this?!"

I paused for a moment then the lightbulb came on. I can't keep living like this. Frustration is wearing me down. I must make this life work, but how? The people and other things on my list weren't the problem. My expectations were. I had standards of excellence and believed in doing things with precision. I'd go above and beyond for people who barely showed up for me. The internal score keeping, and checklist was frustrating me even more. Why was I doing this to myself? People weren't doing anything different than they'd always done. So why in the world was I expecting any different? Why are you expecting any different? People are who and how they are.

Like me, you'll need to adjust your expectations of yourself and others. You choose to be disappointed when you have expectations that people aren't flawed humans. We all make mistakes. We've all hurt or disappointed someone. So why do you expect perfection from other people? People have shown you who and how they are. So far you haven't really believed them, but it's about time you started.

The human factor is too great of an opponent for your expectations so adjust. I make it a habit of adjusting my expectations after each disappointment. I don't allow myself to be disappointed by the same or similar situation twice. You know when a situation is looking too familiar. Instead of getting frustrated, adjust. See people and things for how they are. So, how do you do that?

Change your lens. See your life through a loving, realistic lens, then determine what you can change and act. Focus on the most critical parts. Don't get hyper focused or nitpick. Those things which you can't live without or need to function, are what you should focus on. Beware, don't try to change other people, because it's impossible and will only lead to you being more frustrated. If it's a young child that you are responsible for, then retrain the child. If it's an adult, then practice serenity. Ask God to help you to see, understand, and accept those things which you cannot change. Through understanding comes compassion. Through compassion comes acceptance.

Accept that people and the world will never complete you or be or do enough. They'll never appreciate you enough, love you enough, support you enough, accept you enough, be there for you enough, help you enough, cover you enough, treat you with kindness enough... enough. People, the world, and things will never be or do enough because it's not their job. They are NOT the source of your peace and strength. Just like you, they were never meant to carry such a load. By putting your hope and faith in them, you will be failed every time. Adjust your expectations. Make peace with it and seek a higher source. God is always listening.

Grieve and Let Go

They say in order to live, sometimes you must die, but for me in order to live I had to grieve and let go. After a very overwhelming weekend, I was drained. Things had happened that were near devastating to me and while my natural tendency was to get angry, I DECIDED to respond differently. I cried then released the situation to God. With it came peace. In that moment I knew that I was covered, and He was taking care of the rest.

What made me want to respond differently? I'm glad you asked. I was tired of being tired. Like me, you've reached the point where you can't and won't stand for being emotionally hijacked. You've grown tired of the emotional script that your mind takes you through every time things don't go as planned or when you are disappointed. It's been building up and I know you can feel it. Rather than stuffing and exploding or exploding or

47

venting or stewing silently, let go. Let it all go! Peace can't exist in the same place as pissed off.

Letting go gave me peace, calm, and comfort. When the anger attempted to return, I processed it properly. I wasn't angry, I was hurt. For the first time in a long time, I allowed myself to feel hurt. I allowed myself to feel the emotion I was really feeling instead of the one I was comfortable feeling. When I did, do you know what happened? I didn't come undone! I didn't fall apart. Neither will you. I felt ALL the emotions then released each one to God. It was amazing! The pressure lifted and the tired feeling left. I was free. When you get hurt, the hurt is what is it, but it does NOT define you. Rather than running it through your mind over and over, RELEASE IT! Let Go!

In addition to releasing the hurt masking itself as anger, I took some time to truly grieve my sorrows and to let go of the possibilities. I let go of the life I could've had if I had or had not made certain decisions. I let go of the life I felt I was entitled to or deserved. I let go of the life I had prior to my children, prior to my first husband, prior to my second husband, and prior to my life becoming what it was.

You'll want to let go too. I let go of the disappointment, sadness, guilt, hurt, sorrow, shame, defeat, frustration, and rage. Let go of ALL the things that are holding you back, so that you can start living your best life. Let go of the life that you fantasize about having if you left the one you have. Let go of it all and grieve it all so you can start to really be okay. With every tear you weep, free yourself and get a step closer to being better and living your best life. You won't be able to move forward until you let go. Stop feeling trapped in your life.

Your world is what it was going to be, but you need to be better in order to manage it. You won't even begin to figure out how to make this life work, until you truly give up on what you think you want, need, or deserve. When I say to let go, I don't mean for you to settle or accept a bad life. I'm asking you to adjust your expectations.

The biggest barrier to your future is hanging on to your ideas about your past. The second biggest barrier is your fantasies about the life you could have if things were different. The life you fantasize about running away to if you only had the resources. I'm telling you, no matter how great something or someone looks, everything in life has a cost. Letting go is much healthier and easier than running away.

If you are considering leaving, you also must realize that even if you left today, nothing would be as it was, could've been, or as you envision. The possibilities are dead. Dead things don't come back, so you have to let them go or you'll die with them. Hanging on to dead ideals is like hanging on to the coffin of a loved one as it is lowered into the ground. You must let go or die with them.

You'll find that the sooner you let go of your ideas of the perfect life and focus on the plan for the life you have, the better you'll be. So, grieve and let go, then grieve and let go again. Grieving is an ongoing process, as we pick things up along the journey of life and self-discovery. So, grieve as often as needed, but don't get stuck there. Grieving is cleansing and looks differently from person to person. Some people cry or yell or walk or run or withdraw or attend a retreat or pray or a combination of things. How you grieve is up to you; just let go in a safe space.

Find the best way for you to grieve and let go, like really let go of what is holding you back emotionally and mentally so that you can move forward. Important Note: If you are in immediate hurt, harm, or danger you should leave (when safe to do so) or seek assistance from the proper authorities. No one has to suffer abuse!

Don't let go of things by avoiding them or emotionally checking out. Leaving (emotionally or physically) should NOT be your go to problem solving method for all of life's disappointments. Avoidance will NEVER get you the full release you need, because you are delaying the pain now and saving it for another (usually inconvenient) time.

If you hold back your emotions long enough, you may even convince yourself that you are fine. However, you'll eventually find something or someone that peels the skin off that old wound and then you run the risk of bleeding to death. You may even bleed all over people who didn't hurt you or you'll find yourself back in the same situation over and over again. When you don't deal with an issue, then you can't let it go emotionally.

You're not meant to carry the weight that you do, so it wears you out and breaks you down. Before you know it, you have headaches, insomnia, eating issues (too much or too little), gastrointestinal disorders (stomach problems), weird aches and pains, allergies develop out of nowhere, and other psychosomatic ailments (i.e. physical symptoms that develop in the body, which are caused by emotions or one's thought process rather than have a real physical cause). Pain isn't the part of life you want to face repeatedly. It's one of life's teachers that you want to encounter and learn the lesson from the first time around.

Come to Terms and Get A Grip

Coming to terms was the hardest thing I've ever had to conquer in my life!! Coming to terms means taking responsibility for your life and everything in it. My sense of entitlement made me feel as if I deserved better and if life didn't meet my standards then it needed to change. The truth was I hadn't changed and needed to transform in order to be okay.

The funny thing is I thought I was doing well. I thought that I was living in my truth. The bigger house, the job, the new baby, and how I was going about my life were what I wanted so I should be happy. I mean I prayed for this! However, in praying for what I wanted, I didn't think about the added responsibility. When I was praying for these things, I forgot to pray for the peace and strength to handle the AND in my life.

I often found myself having to come to terms over and over again. There were days when I thought to myself "I got this. I can do this!" Then other days I thought "This is too much AND! Why am I doing all this?" Unfortunately, in the beginning the "This is too much AND" days were the ones that prevailed. Almost daily I found myself having to talk myself into being happy and grateful in this life. Are you constantly convincing yourself to be happy because this is the life you wanted? That you can handle the AND in your life?

Being sure is a struggle, especially when there is extra responsibility.

Do you feel you are where you should be?
A lot   Some   Not At All
Do you feel trapped in your life?
A lot   Some   Not At All

In coming to terms, you learn to live in peace with yourself and your environment. Peace is a decision that only happens with forgiveness. Release a bit each day and you'll find a little more peace. Slowly but surely as you come to terms, you'll gain peace which leads to acceptance. Acceptance isn't agreement or complacency or being stuck. Acceptance means you acknowledge the way things are, you've made a plan for improving things within your control (focus on concrete and critical things), and you've decided to love the hell out of the rest. It's being determined to be happy no matter what!

You can control your life. Focus on what's critical and important, then accept the rest. Yes, things are a mess at times, and they could be 100% better. However, you must accept your life and make it work. Incremental improvements are more sustainable and work best. Be consist and don't give up even if you don't see the progress you feel you should. Transformation is much like weight loss, you might not see the difference at first, but if you stick to it, you'll see where the inches have come off and things are looking pretty good.

Acceptance isn't complacency or being stuck. Acceptance means you know what you have, and while it's not great, it's yours. In making this life work you chose this life and come hell or high water you are dedicated to being happy in it. There is NO other option!

While you are transforming your life, do NOT compare yourself or circumstances to others. No one on earth has a perfect life no matter how great they make it look online.

What you see online is the edited version of what's really going on. Those perfect pictures of their perfect life are just carefully selected snapshots of what they want you to see.

Also, more money won't fix *everything,* and it won't make you happy permanently. Money may improve things, but it won't make you happy if you or your mate must work longer or harder to get it. Children won't make you happy because they are flawed human beings who are constantly changing and learning. A new mate or bae won't make you happy, because that's not his job. People WILL disappoint you so steady yourself and plant yourself firm so that no matter what comes your way, you are healthy, happy, and in a good headspace.

This is your life, you chose it, so learn to love it and make this life work. Start by honestly answering the following questions.

What can you change in your life?

_____

_____

What can you live with or accept for how it is?

_____

_____

What can you do now to make things better?

_____

_____

What can you do now for a better future?

_____

_____

Beware of the Apathy Trap

So, you've done the work, but is this apathy or acceptance? I found myself accepting and accepting and accepting, then one day I was unbothered. Well at least so I thought. It turns out I'd become apathetic and

58

emotionally unavailable. Apathy is "a lack of feeling or emotion; a lack of interest or concern" (Merriam-Webster.com). It's indifference or feeling numb.

I thought I had peace, but the migraines and regular back pain were major indicators that I obviously hadn't really accepted my life. The reality that I needed to accept was I was early into a new marriage and life, plus I'd just started completely over with an infant, I had changed my oldest daughter's life from the baby to an only child to the oldest child, all while trying to advance my career. What was I thinking?!

At least once a week I was having something going on. What are signs that you are not as okay as you think you are? Like me, if someone asks how you are doing you probably say "fine" or "okay." You probably really aren't either, but don't want to get into it. The people closest to you have an idea of how you really are and will eventually say something.

My moment came one day when my Godmother lovingly pulled me aside and told me about myself. She emotionally ran up on me with both hands and slapped my face. She told me that she'd noticed that I'd been saying I was tired all the time, and seemed to be extremely hostile plus short tempered. When she asked me how I was, I responded by saying okay, but she wasn't having it. She kept on me and I agreed to get back to her. At first I was offended like "how dare she come over here with that? I'm fine!" Then my ego stepped aside, and I really thought it through. Was I really okay, or was I just pretending?

When I took a hard look at myself, I had to finally admit that I wasn't okay. I couldn't take anymore AND so instead of fixing the problem, I stop caring. I had checked out emotionally. I thought I was "unbothered" and had finally accepted my new normal, but I didn't give two dead flies about what was going on in my life. I was just existing and going through the motions.

In moving from apathy to true acceptance, I had to first admit to myself how I really felt. I had to own my truth that this wasn't going exactly like I had in mind. I figured this was my do over so it should be PERFECT! I imagined a President Barack and First Lady Michelle Obama power couple combo. I'm talking me and him against the world; him loving and covering me from the top of my head to the tip of my toes. I got that, but the AND that came with it was overwhelming.

With acceptance I embraced the humanness of my husband, my kids, and myself. This experience didn't come with instructions and even if there were instructions, they weren't one size fits all. We would have to figure it all out without causing irreputable harm to one another or our kids.

Acceptance isn't checking out or disconnecting; that's apathy. It's not allowing your emotions to fester under the surface, while painting on the "I'm fine" face. True peace and acceptance won't leave you feeling numb or not caring or indifferent. You'll feel free, joyous, calm, and not sweating the small stuff. When you really have peace and acceptance, you'll let things go and not pick them back up.

Tips for Letting Go and Getting a Grip:
1. Be honest with yourself about where you are emotionally, financially, parentally, spiritually, relationship wise, etc.
2. Re-evaluate your values and priorities
3. Be realistic in your expectations of others and yourself
4. Quickly accept the little things and let them go, so that they don't grow and become a big deal

Chapter 3:
Drop The Drama

Feelings are not dictators so stop allowing them to hijack your life. -- Dr. Chris Hubbard Jackson

Waking up each day, seeing the sun rise is a cleansing, calming experience used to steady the mind. For a long time, it reminded me of yet another day of things to do. I spent YEARS feeling emotionally, mentally, and physically tired of everything I had to be accountable for in my life, but you don't have to. You can get out of the perpetual state of dissatisfaction, discouragement, and disappointment. Just drop the internal drama and make this life work. YOU get to decide!

There will always be things to do and things left undone, but YOU get to decide how you feel. YOU can have an overwhelmed, fed-up outlook or you can have a blessed, balanced, breakthrough outlook. The day is what it is in all its misery or glory, and the best part is YOU get to decide. You can take the glass half empty approach or better yet, you can drink the wine and savor it instead of whining about how small the glass is. Just refill, sip, savor, and repeat.

Feeling like "this is that foolishness" may come upon you, often accompanied by a physical ailment such as an upset stomach, a headache/migraine, weird aches, and odd pains. However, you don't have to accept the thought and best of all you don't have to suffer through it. I often say, "it is what it is, so keep it moving," not as a point of apathy, but rather as a point of acceptance. I use such clichés to keep from getting bogged down by emotional drama.

Let's explore that. You get frustrated when you internalize words, situations, and information, that should just be acknowledged in a passive "yeah okay" kind of way. Just think about it for a moment. How much energy do you waste on processing information using your feelings, rather than just acknowledging it rationally and letting it go?

You don't have to have deep feelings about something for it to be important. For example, that project you are working on is important and will take a lot of work, but you don't have to feel overwhelmed by it. If it produces an emotional reaction such as irritation, sympathy, frustration, eye rolling, crying, or anger; take a moment to really think about your response. Is your response appropriate and will it help to improve the situation? Usually the answer is "NO", so don't waste your energy. Drop the drama. The drama only drains you.

The next time you encounter information, pay attention to your response. What part of the information triggers anxiety? For instance, is your heart racing, are your hands sweating or clammy, is your breathing different? Now also think about the details surrounding your response. Was internalizing that experience beneficial, and did it encourage you? I'm guessing probably not. That thought or those words, were never meant to make it inside of you.

You allowed VIP access to general information. Just like people you see from time to time, general information shouldn't have VIP access and for good reason. It's because allowing general information past a certain internal point is an emotional security risk. Unnecessary emotional responses are discouraging and will likely get you emotionally hijacked. Don't allow situations or information to run off with your emotions. Don't do it to yourself!

You say, "Chris I'm good to go on that, I'm drama free." Okay, but are you really? Have you checked your heart? Drop the drama does not mean to pretend to be okay on the outside while being a smoking hot mess with no eyelashes and no edges on the inside. No ma'am, there is no faking that and you can't fake it with yourself. If you are easily offended or wrinkle your face in response to information, you are not as drama free as you might think.

Drop the drama means to control your emotions and thoughts. It's speaking encouragement into yourself. It's ensuring that you are focusing on the positive rather than being fixated on the negative. It's interrupting the thoughts that weigh you down, by replacing them with positive thoughts. Each negative thought that attempts to cross your mind, must be interrupted by three to five repetitions of the same positive thought or three to five positive thoughts in a row. Push out the drama!

Encourage Yourself

Be your own hype woman. Encourage yourself! Where's your theme music? Every woman needs theme music such as "Hate On Me Haters" by Jill Scott, or "Roar" by Katy Perry. Your theme music is your let's get moving music. It's your positive, uplifting, empowering music. You also may want a bit of soul reaching music. Songs like "Close" by Marvin Sapp, "Not Today Satan" by KB, or "Surrounded" by Michael W. Smith. On those days when your internal encouragement isn't enough, you need to have songs or sermons or something that gets you up and moving.

Keep moving by keeping a constant source of motivation. What your mind is exposed to helps shape your reality. I found that if I stayed away from church or didn't listen to gospel or didn't listen to sermons or uplifting messages throughout my day, I felt drained. Each day felt like a fight for my life! I had to figure out how to arm myself because I was fighting for my future and my purpose.

What you put in becomes your foundation, and when you are under fire it becomes your default response. In being encouraged you'll want to surround yourself with people, messages, and music which uplift your spirits. When I felt down, I had people pray with me and for me. I sought out encouragement daily. Despite my efforts, something was missing.

I kept having this feeling deep down on the inside of being overwhelmed and empty. I was lost and didn't know how to find myself. I knew something wasn't right, but I didn't have the energy to figure out what or any idea of how to get myself together. I was all over the place. Sometimes I had hope, other times I had despair or emptiness, then I'd be ready to take on the world, but would get overwhelmed. I was functional on the outside, but on the inside I was a hot mess.

One day it finally occurred to me that until I dealt with my inner turmoil, I could never truly be encouraged. This started with a conversation with God. I then learned how to properly process my emotions. When something upset or angered me, I'd ask myself why I was angry or upset, what really was making me feel that way, and if what I was feeling was legitimate.

There are times when your feelings betray or trick you into thinking things are wrong when the situation doesn't require the response you are having. Feelings will have you in a constant state of angst or anxiety if you let them. Don't get emotionally hijacked. The ride isn't free and includes way more twists and turns than any reasonable person can handle. You'll have to rewire your emotions; especially if your first response is an emotional one.

How do you know if your emotions are driving you? Look for these signs. Feeling flushed or warm when you encounter information you disagree with. Feeling exhausted or like you've been punched, after a conversation. Disconnecting from the facts when you are confronted. Escalating or intensifying disagreements with others. If any of these descriptions sound like your typical response, you are well on your way to being emotionally hijacked. Once your emotions start driving in a situation, being hijacked is easy.

If you don't have a proper foundation, your default will be negative self-talk. The worries will rise up and the fear can paralyze you. The doubt and "what if" scenarios of failure will replay over and over in your head until they are the only thing you can think of and hear. Silence your own thoughts. Fix and replace your internal script. You are in charge of your brain's narrative and you don't have to accept just any thought that crosses your mind. If your thoughts are on a negative loop, then you can't properly control your emotions.

Emotions operate by pattern and default. You'll face the same five to seven struggles over and over, just in different seasons and in newer ways. Don't be fooled. That same challenge you faced at five will appear at 10, 15, 20, and on again until death. Also beware of familiar traps disguised as new people. As you mature and grow, so will your challenges, which is why being encouraged often is critical. You will learn how to defeat the things you've faced previously and recognize when those things have changed into a challenge on a higher level. Staying encouraged in spite of your challenges is critical but can be tricky at times. Stay alert!

The funny thing about encouragement is it can show up in the strangest places or ways. Don't disregard a message just because the messenger is in a less than desirable or unexpected package. Wisdom and guidance can come from the strangest places and situations. For example, I was having a rough morning and my youngest was being uncooperative. As I was putting her into the car, I put my purse on the top of the car. I turned a couple of corners and exited my subdivision. As I turned onto a busy street, my brand-new purse flew off the top of my car. Mind you I'd gotten cash the night before to pay the daycare.

I quickly put the car in park and hurriedly picked up the contents of my now scuffed-up purse. A few people stopped to help me, which I appreciated. I got to the daycare and guess what I couldn't find? You guessed it, the money. My older daughter said, "Mom, how much money is missing and what will you do?!" I looked her in the face and calmly said "It is what it is. Getting upset changes nothing. I'll look for the money later. I must get to work."

I could've gotten upset or gotten emotionally hijacked, but I decided to keep my peace instead. The situation taught me that life happens, especially when you are in a hurry. So rather than getting upset about the things you can't control or change, slow down and breathe. It'll be okay. I did, and as I started to put the contents of my purse back into place, I found the money, carefully tucked away and undisturbed.

Forgive Daily

Another way to drop the drama is through forgiveness. Forgiveness is the greatest gift you can give yourself. Yet since we are so selfless it is the hardest thing for us to do. When most people hear forgiveness or forgive, they tend to roll their eyes. It's because forgiveness has been given a bad rap as a passive "let people walk all over you" kind of tactic. I'm here to tell you, that's not what forgiveness is at all. Forgiveness doesn't mean you must allow people to hurt you. Forgiveness don't mean you must keep dealing with the people who hurt you. Forgiveness is definitely NOT a clean slate of wrongdoing or a get out of jail free card for wrong doers.

Forgiveness means you drop the drama and let go of what the person did to you. It's freeing yourself from pain by emotionally letting go and not being offended. It's letting go of the hurt, anger, bitterness, and suffering associated with the wrong. It's making the hurt and person powerless over your life. As Louise L. Hay so eloquently put it, "When you forgive and let go, not only does a huge weight drop off your shoulders, but the doorway to your own self-love opens."

When someone does you wrong, you owe it to *yourself* to forgive them because if you don't, they maintain power over your emotions. Emotional people are unstable and easy to manipulate, especially when you know what pushes their buttons. If you've ever hurt someone you have a clue into the right buttons and that's dangerous. By pushing the right buttons people willingly do strange things or act out of character, which they'll probably regret. This gives more power to the offender and causes further spiraling down the crazy hole. Let's not end up in the sunken place.

When you forgive people, you don't have to deal with them or even tell them that you have forgiven them. You can forgive and not deal with them, but you must not harbor any ill will or resentment. See, that's the key and the trickiest part. Let's explore that for a moment. You can't say I forgive you, but if you were on fire, I wouldn't spit on you to put you out. That's not forgiveness by any stretch of the imagination.

With forgiveness you might see the person on fire and feel nothing toward their circumstances. In most cases you won't even notice they are burning unless someone brings it to your attention. You could even start to feel bad for the person's suffering (for most of us this usually isn't the case, but it could happen).

So how do you know that you've forgiven, and your heart is whole? If the hurt is still there you truly have NOT forgiven. How do you know if the hurt is still there? If you talk about a situation and it causes an emotional response, then you are still holding on to it. For instance, if at the mention of the person's name you tell people how they hurt or offended you or did you wrong, you have not forgiven. If you randomly replay exchanges you've had with the person, and the memories are upsetting, you have not forgiven. No matter the harm done, forgiveness is absolutely necessary in order to free yourself.

What is needed in order to forgive, will determine which response is appropriate. It will vary from offender to offender. When you forgive you will let go of any ill will, wish them well and let karma do its job. Karma is a beast and she's great at collecting on debts with interest. So, don't worry, they don't get away free and clear, but your mind and heart will be. Free yourself because no other help is coming. No one can free you from this but you. Don't wait on the other person to apologize and don't think a confrontation will get you the happy ending you desire. Forgive without expectations or conditions.

Forgiveness soothes the soul, calms the mind, and eases the nerves. It took me quite some time to realize how much unforgiveness was hiding in my heart. Bitterness, anger, resentment, hurt, rage, and apathy are ALL symptoms of the same problem, and it is unforgiveness. You say, "Chris I'm not much for second chances, but I don't consider myself a die-hard grudge holder either. Plenty of people in my life have hurt or disappointed me and I'm doing just fine because I've let that go."

That may be the case for those you don't have much contact with, but for those you still must deal with, it's a monumental task. Those who are close to you or at one time or another had been close to you, have some offenses that you are still holding on to. It is like everything they do is an add-on to previous hurt that they have caused. For instance, you are working on an important project with a few co-workers who don't complete their part of the project. As a result, you stay up all night finishing the project. From then on you don't trust them and every time you need them to complete a task you bring up the fact that they didn't do their part on that one project. Working with them makes you feel stressed and annoyed. While you say you have let it go, you truly haven't.

Unforgiveness makes you toxic and your emotions eventually will start to leak out. Meanwhile you are the one who is coming undone and the people who did you wrong probably haven't even noticed. Even worse, a few that have noticed, probably don't care or blame you for the situation. Why give them the power and satisfaction of seeing you miserable? You've given them enough!

I know you're thinking that if they'd just apologize or if they'd stop doing stuff then you could forgive. At one point I fell into the proverbial "they" trap. If they would just... If they would stop... If they, if they, if they... After a while I got tired of hearing my own whining and decided to do something about it. They will probably never apologize, and you must forgive in spite of. Forgiveness is NEVER about the other person. Forgiveness is ALL about reclaiming YOUR peace and healing the scars the offense left on YOUR heart.

Who has wronged you and what did they do?

_____

_____

How did what they did impact you?

_____

_____

Is the hurt worth holding on to?

Yes   No

Do you want the relationship with the person?

Yes   No

Forgiveness Strategies

My first reaction to unforgiveness was to go through the list of wrongs in my mind then confront those who had done me wrong. I started with people who I had more of a distant or casual relationship with. I quickly learned that approach was an epic disaster. Most of the people on my list either didn't realize they had done anything or didn't care. In a few situations I felt worse than before we talked, and ended the relationship. My second approach was to talk through each of these issues with a trusted friend and I found that this just led to more whining and complaining.

My third approach and the one I would recommend to you is to make a list of the wrongs and pray or mediate on each one. You'll want to ask that your heart is willing and able to release the offenses. With time and understanding, you'll let go of a little bit each day. You'll determine which things truly need conversations and which things you can let go of without communicating with the other person.

This process took me some time because I had so much stored up. I had a notepad of the wrongs and about 10 pages in I realized that I shouldn't have allowed this much to get stored in my heart. Yes 10 legal sized pages of a lifetime of wrong. Some days of prayer and forgiveness led to tears, while others led to praise. I resolved that with each release, I wouldn't allow those things to return nor would I allow new offenses to take root. I breezed through my list of low and mid-level offenders, but that top level of offenders was going to take some work.

Forgive For Real

The top offenders were made up of five important people in my life who were still impacting my life in some way. They should've been people who protected and loved me unconditionally, but they used our relationship for selfish gain. The interesting thing about the top five was that the offenses they were accused of were things they had in common. They had violated my trust, and showed no real remorse for their wrongdoing.

Tackling them all at once would have been sudden death, so I dealt with the top offender first. For you, dealing with the least of them will work better so I encourage you to do that if that works best for you. Now before you go and shoot up people's emotional houses, you should strongly consider what you really want to gain here.

Is talking to them worth it? What will you gain?

_____

_____

What will you lose and is losing it worth what you hope to gain?

_____

_____

Will doing this give you peace or cause more hurt for you?

_____

_____

I'm not afraid of confrontation so I wanted to get the worst of the worst, out of the way first. In dealing with the top offender, I thought and prayed until I could clearly articulate to myself (with examples) of what exactly London (name changed for privacy) had done wrong. London was a user and had shown me that every time I'd let my guard down with him. London had played on my sympathy and exploited it for personal gain.

I took the offenses to God and asked him to heal my heart. I then attempted to talk to the top offender, but London was unable to even admit any wrong had been done. London even insisted on being a victim in the situations named. I was floored, irritated and exhausted by the end. However, I was determined to get it off me, so I didn't give up. I said what I needed to say. I told London all was forgiven and moved on.

For some reason this act triggered a "let's reconnect" attempt from London, but I wasn't going for the foolishness. No ma'am I had no interest in having a deeper relationship because London had already proven to be out for self-interests at whatever cost. I was determined to NOT be fooled again so I had to pray some more in order to determine what boundaries needed to be put in place.

I determined that we could have casual conversations and interactions in passing, but that was all that the relationship would be. In forgiveness I found a major level of peace. Untangling all that came with that relationship was a growth experience which helped prepare me for the other four.

The second top offender had put me through hell. Alex (name changed for privacy) was abusive mentally, physically, and financially. After gaining my trust, Alex treated me like property. I had no choice but to end the relationship. However, Alex would still popup from time to time, despite being unwanted. I'd encountered too many years of foolishness and I had no interest in having conversations with him. I took ALL my cares and issues concerning my unforgiveness, to God and let it go. I released my forgiveness into the atmosphere and placed any hurt under my feet. I would no longer allow this hurt to control me. It wasn't worth it and quite frankly Alex didn't care or maybe even found joy in my suffering. I refused to give anyone that kind of power over me, so I had to let go. I evicted Alex from my life, but it was critical that I evict him from my heart, so out it all went.

The third top offender was the person I had the most difficulty forgiving. Bailey (name changed for privacy) was a constant offender. Bailey would attempt to manipulate and set me off in order to play the victim. I thought avoidance would be the key, but that failed. I thought pushing Bailey away would work, but that failed too. I tried being mean, I tried being nice, I tried being indifferent, but nothing worked.

Finally, I tried forgiveness, but not before the confrontation. Bailey and I went around and around and around, but with no resolve. I expressed the harm and hurt she had caused, but her response was to tell me about the hurt and harm I'd caused. Before long I was exhausted, and I was sick of it. I instead resolved to cast each and every care on God. I let it all go. I also asked for clarity on dealing with Bailey. Boundary setting ended up being the key. I decided I was going to put firm boundaries in place, and I would be on guard for Bailey's attempts to circumvent them. I would also forgive daily because daily forgiveness means daily restoration.

Dealing with offenders one through three was so exhausting that by the time I made it to four and five it was easy. Offender number four and I talked. We both shared our views on the issues between us. I felt Tory (name changed for privacy) had been disloyal, and Tory felt abandoned. We both apologized and committed to doing better. We established ground rules for the relationship and have been great ever since.

Offender number five didn't require a conversation, but rather just forgiveness on my part. Based on prior interactions I knew Frankie (name changed for privacy) couldn't handle the exchange, so I just let it go. I'd been hurt by people he brought into my life. The harm had been done over the duration of our relationship, and it wasn't until I went in search of myself, that I mentioned it to anyone. I knew Frankie didn't understand all that was done and nothing that happened was he hadn't brought those people into my life with malicious intent. Letting go was the best gift I gave myself and forgiving others is a great gift for you too!

In addition to forgiving those who have done you wrong, you also must forgive yourself. Forgive yourself for allowing it to happen, for not speaking up soon enough, for not realizing the harm that unforgiveness was causing, and for not putting proper boundaries in place sooner. You need *your* forgiveness more than anyone else. You are worth it!

Remember, the point in forgiveness isn't for the other person, but instead for your peace. You can't have a clean heart and inner peace until you let go of ALL the things that are holding you back. Letting go can be difficult, but holding on is even harder. Choose you, instead of the hurt. Choose your sanity, your peace, your wholeness, and your joy. There is no shortage of suffering and hurt in this word. Peace on the other hand is a gift that you must work for. I hope you choose to spend a little of each day forgiving and letting go. Maintain your peace, rather than suffering.

Forgiveness is something I do daily and has served me well. If I don't let go of something, I find that after a few days I'm bogged down, tired and ineffective. Being drained or constantly tired without a physical cause, is a clue that you are harboring unforgiveness. Let go and stop killing yourself. Drop the drama and be free.

Tips for Dropping the Drama:

1. Decide to stop being offended
2. Encourage yourself often
3. Forgive daily
4. Forgive yourself

Chapter 4:
Put Your Mission Where Your Mouth Is

"The words of the reckless pierce like swords, but the tongue of the wise brings healing." Proverbs 12:18 NIV

Every January you see the commercials and advertisements for gym memberships. The first two months of the year, gyms are packed, but by March just about every machine in the gym is available. You and I both know why that is. People are good at talking and acting like they want better, but do they really?! In some areas of my life, I've been that way. How about you? For instance, I want to look toned and fit, but I also want to eat recklessly on days when my emotions get the better of me. Plus, I dislike working out because it hurts.

Where is the movement that matches your mouth? How determined are you? For some getting started is the hardest, while for others staying determined is the true test. For me, it's a combination depending on the task. Determination is an uphill battle that at times may feel like you are rolling backwards or not moving at all or maybe even just running in place. Let me be clear, movement for movement's sake isn't progress, it's restlessness. Staying determined entails pushing and P.U.S.H.ing (praying until something happens) forward until you get the desired results.

Determination is as much a test of the mind, energy, and focus, as it is a test of ability. Good things don't come easy and achieving great things will test you. Anything you gain easily will often be taken for granted. It's like when you give kids something without making them work for it. They don't value it! The sticking strength you gain during the process is just as important as the result.

Staying determined means putting and keeping your purpose in front of you. It's continuing to move forward despite what things look like. It's recognizing that your success in life is a journey so you must stay determined to be who it is that you are called to be. It won't be easy, but you are more than worth it. You say, "Chris what if I fail?" Okay, but even failure requires taking steps. Show up for YOU!

All my life I have excelled, but for others this may be quite the opposite. Everyone will eventually fail at something, but the funny thing about failure is people only teach you how to win. They don't teach you how to fail with grace. Divorcing my first husband was the first time in my life I had failed, and I failed hard. I mean I had experienced quick loses such as not winning first place at something, but I always came back to dominate. I had experienced not getting the grade I wanted, but this made me work harder for it. However, no one EVER prepared me for failing publicly and for an extended period of time. I was surprised by what was happening to me and I didn't know how I was going to keep going, but I did.

I focused on the plan instead of the pain and I got through it. Getting over it wasn't an option. Getting through it was my ONLY option. It looks like the only option for you too. I learned that even at my weakest, God could find a way to send me strength. When I focused on the problems I was drained. When I focused on God and obeyed those internal prompts that maintained my peace, I found understanding that nothing in this world could give me. Also, in failing, I saw my true myself. I was alone with my thoughts and too embarrassed to seek guidance. On top of it, I had kids to consider. What was I going to do?

I attempted to wallow in self-pity and shame, but that didn't fix the problem. So, I did the only thing I could do! I got control of myself and my emotions, affirmed myself, sought out resources to correct my deficiencies, and built the next, newer, better version of myself. You can too!

How do you stay determined when quitting seems like an easier plan? Your determination is something that is impacted internally and externally. What's inside of you is what you can control so focus on that. Treat you and your goals with the same dignity and care, as someone you highly respect and or love. Become determined not to fail YOU. Make yourself a priority! Begin by helping YOU.

What was meant to break you can build you up, if you let it! You can gain a skillset that you might not gain any other way. Own your determination rather than letting it be something that is subjected to the will of others or your environment. Make your determination a part of who you are. Determination, resilience, restoration, peace, and grace will become your joy and strength.

Make up your mind that no matter what comes at you (life will indeed come at you with both hands) you will NOT allow anything or anyone to steal your determination from you.

You can only be defeated if you give up! Life is going to be what it will be, and you can use your free will to impact life for the better or for the worse. However, at the end of the day, when you look back and reflect on all that has occurred, even when you were down you were not defeated unless you gave up! You can only be defeated if you give up. Giving up includes stopping or not putting in the energy and effort needed to propel you forward, or not starting at all.

If starting seems overwhelming, then begin with the end in mind. Ask yourself, "What do my perfect world and a perfect me look like?" Now back your way into it. How can you get there? What skills, resources, and connections do you need? What can you do today to get moving? Go do that. What can you do this week? Now go do that. What can you do this month? Next month? Within 90 days? Within six months? Within a year?

A year from now is a year from now so you can either be closer to your dream or still having a pity party about not being able to get there. You and your determination get to choose. It's 100% up to you regardless of the obstacles you face. You can hear "NO" a million times, but it only takes the right "Yes" at the right time, to change your life. "NO" isn't a rejection but instead an option to search for other opportunities or ways to get you to where you want to be.

Transformation Is Worth It

So, what keeps me determined? The vision of my best me and my best life keep me determined and moving. Plus, I believe that stealing is wrong, so I won't help anyone steal from me. I won't give the world my purpose or my peace or my joy. So, what if you don't know what your best version of you looks like and what your best life looks like? Then look and plan for it.

What are some habits or personality quirks that you have which are less than great? Start with the ones you know. You know the ones I'm talking about. I'm talking about the ones you have been told repeatedly that you need to fix. The qualities that you may have even accepted as being "part of who you are." Let's be clear, any habit or quality that stands in the way of your progress is a firm "NO," and needs to be fixed. No excuses and no attempts to justify. Don't kid yourself into thinking that's just who you are.

Another clue to what needs to change is those traits which used to be effective defense mechanisms, but are now wreaking havoc in your life. For instance, anger was a major go to for me, because my anger got stuff done. For over 25 years anger picked me up and kept me moving when I couldn't even lift my head from the pillow in my own strength. However, at this point, it's a distraction and destructive problem, because it has caused resistance by others who are able to help me. People help people they like, and ignore or hurt people they dislike.

Now I'm not saying you must be liked by everyone or change who you are every 15 seconds. What I am saying is that being pleasant, and likeable is helpful in removing barriers and getting things done. Knowing who you are is critical to adapting your behavior as needed. When you know who you are, you recognize that minor adjustments aren't major personality changes and don't make you "fake." Adjusting is a sign of emotional maturity. To know yourself is to know your truth. Take a moment to consider these questions.

What qualities define you?

_____

_____

What traits do you have that are strong indicators of who you are?

_____

_____

What are your best character traits?

_____

_____

I was forced to re-evaluate myself. After having the toughest 90 days of my life, I broke and fell hard into despair. During that time, I or people close to me had lost five loved ones, including the loss of one of my best friends. Losing her made me question everything I knew about death and challenged my relationship with God. I was hurt, angry, sad, and unmotivated. Doing nothing was even exhausting because when I laid my head on the pillow to rest, I'd start thinking about everything I didn't have the strength to do.

For a while I ignored God because how dare He take my friend from me, her children, her husband, and this world without at least giving me time to get ready. I was prideful, entitled, and broken. Being the go-to person, I was able to help with the arrangements. However, once things were done, my brain crashed and my energy went with it.

I didn't take the time off from work I needed to, and I still had to deal with my own family. It got to be too much, and I broke. I humbled myself before God, poured out my hurt, anger, and frustration then slowly began to heal. In making this life work I had to deal with myself and work things out with God so that I could move through all this tragedy instead of allowing life to derail me. Since life was too much for me to tackle on my own, my faith became essential.

Nothing in this world can explain all the tragedy that has pushed you over, knocked you down, and is standing on your chest. Nothing! Despite ALL this, you need to breathe, and you need to heal. Through healing you will develop a determination that you haven't had before. Each day you get a step closer to death and death is a brutal reminder that life is frail. There is no clear end date so you must live each day on purpose and to the fullest. Become determined to live your best life so that even if you die tomorrow, the world owes you nothing. Use your determination to keep yourself motivated to experience the best that life has to offer. Leave your mark on this world and make this life work.

Watch Your Mouth

What is the mission for your life? I mean what are you truly striving for? Take a moment and think. Write it down, flesh it out, and live it out. Your mission is your purpose and determines the direction for your life. Your mission is supported by your values. Values are your core beliefs which help to support and explain your mission. What goals and actions accompany your mission? Take the time to really think on these things then act on them. Update your mission, values, and actions every three to five years. Stay active, keep moving, and don't quit.

What is the mission for your life?

_____

_____

What are your values?

_____

_____

What goals and actions support your mission?

_____

_____

At first matching my mouth with my mission was a foreign concept to me because I didn't understand the power of my words. Like they say, "sticks and stones may break my bones, but words will never hurt me." That is the biggest lie of all and especially in adulthood! Words hurt and will knock the wind out of you quicker than being slugged with a baseball bat. Words will cut you wider and deeper than the most skilled surgeon trying to remove all that ales you. Trust me I know from being the recipient and assailant of unkind words. Words hurt and stick with you long after any physical pain has gone.

Words may be the only memory people have of you once you've been removed from their presence. For years to come people will speak from hurt words from 20 years ago as if it happened that day. Your mouth is one of your biggest weapons and strengths. When you use words to chew people up for breakfast and spit them out for lunch, you are leaving the sting behind to repeat over and over in the person's mind. It whittles away at their self-esteem and their opinion of you.

However, your words can also help you to build others up and to talk yourself out of trouble or into opportunities. How you wield your words is up to you. Your words can be for peace making or peace disturbing.

When I began studying the power of my words, I realized how important they were and decided to control them so they would no longer control me. I had to speak life into my circumstances and affirm the direction of my life so that I'd know each day where I was headed. I'm sure you are wondering how I did it. How'd I learn to match my mouth with my mission?

I became aware of what I said. No really, I realized that much of my internal and external dialog was on autopilot. That with my experiences I had learned to respond certain ways without thinking. When I became more aware and weighed the pros and cons of my words, I started using them wisely.

I also learned to be appropriately silent. No response is a very clear response. In addition to not saying anything unless I had to, I learned to use the most powerful statement of them all... "OH OKAY." That's right, "Oh okay." "Oh okay" means that I heard what you said and I'm choosing not to engage. It is not a sign of agreement, but rather a sign to yourself that you are not going to engage in whatever this is. "Oh okay" puts the mind at ease rather than in a fight or flight let me get ready to defend myself sort of state.

In making this life work you'll learn to match your mouth with your mission by ensuring your words match what you are aspiring to. How you want your life to be is what you should speak. Don't ignore the obvious or lie about your circumstances, but rather focus on the positive in spite of the negative. There may be plenty of negativity along the way, but you don't have to speak on it because it's already done.

Why waste words or time on dead topics? What's done is done and talking about your thoughts or feelings concerning the topic won't fix it, so move along quickly. When you critique what's wrong, you're wasting words and time, which are both too precious to lend to trivial things. Simple as that.

Your words and attitude are an indication of your faith. Your words clearly show your attitude, and could be working against you. Your very own words could be defeating you. As a kid my grandmother used to tell me that everything that crossed my mind shouldn't cross my lips. I didn't understand it then, but it's a concept that I've embraced. I'm teaching my children that everything that crosses their mind shouldn't cross their face or lips. You may want to consider this too. Especially the face part. I bet like me your face responds so that you don't have to.

Some thoughts are processing thoughts, while others are directional thoughts. Processing thoughts are used to sort through information. The processing thoughts should be quick, in and out thoughts. The directional thoughts are used to guide your words and actions. The directional thoughts should cross your mind, and some may cross your lips, guiding you into the direction that you should go. The directional thoughts feed your purpose, and *not* your sense of entitlement. These are words of affirmation, words of support, words of clarity, and words of internal truth which serve as your guide.

Negative thoughts might start to cross your mind or face, but you must interrupt them before they make it to your lips. Train your brain to have a copilot. Mine says things such as "Don't say that. Don't respond to that. Oh okay. Don't go there. Don't stop; keep going, keep going, keep going. Don't stop moving. I'm worth it!" Practice makes perfect in this area. You must train yourself to say "NO," "NO, I'm not going there. NO, I won't judge. NO, I won't complain. NO, I won't give that any thought." Just "NO, Nope, Not today!"

When re-training your thoughts and words it might seem like all of a sudden you get bombard with foolishness. I'm talking like grade A foolishness, that may leave you feeling like this is too much. Instead of going in, on the inside tell yourself "NO!" Over and over as often as needed to interrupt the thought before it gets out of your mouth. If you start to react to foolishness, just pause and interrupt the words by becoming silent or saying, "never mind I don't need to go there."

Notice that when you try to do better some people will test you so stay ready! In making this life work you'll have to turn your mouth's filter all the way up, constantly monitor your thoughts and words, until the new behavior becomes your new normal. Transformation is one day at a time and one word or thought at a time.

In making this life work learn to use your words to attract what you want rather than fueling what you don't want. Even when cringe worthy situations present themselves, refuse to get baited in. Don't speak on it because obvious foolishness usually gets you a ride on the petty bus. Also, be more mindful of what you hear and see. You may want to block a few people from your social media as you gain a new self-awareness. Speak about the positive and learn to be silent when there is nothing positive to speak on. Silence speaks louder than anything.

Matching your mouth to your mission includes speaking as you want others to see you. You can reshape other people's impressions of you by being positive, not speaking on the small stuff, and by becoming verbally mature.

Tips for Matching Your Mouth to Your Mission:

1. Just start (yes, today!)
2. Watch your mouth and your face
3. Don't get baited in
4. Be positive or be silent or say "Oh okay"

Chapter 5:
Treasure Your Tribe

Why You Need A Tribe

"Behind every successful woman is a tribe of other successful women who have her back."
--Author Unknown.

Every woman needs a tribe of other successful women, to help make her life work. You say, "No Chris, I got this!" Do you really? Okay, but for how long? Putting on your Superwoman cape may work for a while, but eventually you'll get tired and ineffective. Doing it ALL on your own will cause you to burn out and break down or quit or become ineffective. You also need a tribe because women understand other women. Even when you're being petty, there's at least one other woman willing to cosign your pettiness.

You'll want to find women who speak your language and vibe on the same wavelength as you. You know the ones. The women that you can talk to without saying a word. You lock eyes and have an entire conversation from across the room. The women who understand what you didn't say, just as much as what you did say. Those women are your tribe. You just have to find the right ones. I'm telling you, finding your tribe is the best thing you can ever do.

You say, "I know, but Chris I don't like women. They are messy. I've been hurt and stabbed in the back." Yes, *those* women did *those* things. I've been hurt by women too and I'm sure there are women who may say the same about me or you. However, if you think about it, you've also been loved, supported, and embraced by at least one woman at some point in your life. Really think about it. So maybe it's not ALL women, but rather the women drawn to you.

What type of women are you attracting and why?

_____

_____

What are the characteristics of the women who are drawn to you? Are they empowering, talkative, gossipers, powerful, mean, nice, strong, etc.?

_____

_____

The women in your tribe speak volumes about you and your character. I'm sure you've heard the old saying "birds of a feather, flock together," and "you never see eagles hanging with pigeons." All of this is true so choose your tribe wisely.

Tackling the AND in life is much easier with a tribe, so don't be the one who always gives, but never receives. Don't convince yourself that the amount of suffering you can handle on your own, somehow makes you enough or better. Don't take on the role of the martyr, suffering for the sake of others. It will wear you down. Seek out other women to be a part of your tribe, who are willing AND able to help. Trust them enough to help you to make your life work. In order for a tribe to be helpful, you must be willing to reciprocate or give as well as take. Ask for help, accept the help, and offer help. You must be okay giving and receiving help without being bothered by it.

Building Your Tribe

When building your tribe remember, not every woman will have the same skill set, and she shouldn't. You want different women with their own unique qualities, benefits, skills, perks, and quirks. Maybe this friend helps pick up the kids. Maybe this one is good at meal prepping. Maybe this one is a great reference for situations with the kids. Maybe this one has great career advice. Maybe this one has great spiritual advice. Maybe this one has great legal advice. The list of women in your tribe goes on and on. So, let's get you a tribe.

A great tribe will have about five women in it, other than you. Each one should add something to you, and you should add something to her. You shouldn't be in a tribe of women you have to constantly comfort and fix. Friends aren't projects so they shouldn't be treated as fixer uppers. You also shouldn't be the woe is me, poor thing, squeaky wheel, in constant need of assistance or care. A woman who is always needy is never a good tribe member.

Tribe membership is giving and taking as needed, without being a burden. If you're constantly asking for help, you may want to consider re-evaluating your life to see what needs to change or stop. Maybe you are over committed or have too much going on. Maybe it's a change in your processes, or that you need to figure out how to be more efficient.

Take a moment to make your list of five women. If you don't have five, then start with three. They can be whoever is willing and available to help. If you still can't come up with five, then list the skills you need and seek women out with those skills.

Name 5 women and at least 3 skills or benefits each woman has.

_____

_____

_____

_____

_____

Some of the women in your tribe will be longtime friends or family. Some may be former coworkers or older ladies from church.

Some may be your sorority sisters or women from other professional organizations. I do want to caution you about selecting people you currently work with. If being in your tribe could put your job or safety at risk, I strongly suggest that you steer clear.

Here's who is in my tribe. One of my best friends is a woman I met by happen stance, while another I have been friends with since childhood. One of my closest friends is a woman I was introduced to by someone else but put off meeting. Another close friend is the wife of a friend. Another is a former coworker. Each woman has her own unique skills and each woman has a special place in my tribe.

Where and when on your journey you met the women in your tribe is irrelevant. The important point is you both provide each other with something the other needs and have a clear understanding of the boundaries of the relationship. And yes, boundaries are critical.

Not one person should know where all your bones are buried.

The women waiting to join your tribe are there. You must reach out to them. Yes, I said YOU. Is there a small group of women that you know that you could join? You don't have to build your tribe from nothing.

You say, "Chris what about my husband or mate or bae or boo?" How does he contribute to my tribe? Where does he fit in? Why do I need a tribe when I have him? Great questions. Like most people, I assumed that if you are married you have an instant partner to share equally in the household responsibilities and duties. That's true, but your partner can't handle everything you're unable to. Sometimes you both need help from other people. For instance, in emergencies, for date night, for couple vacations, and other events.

While you are building your tribe, don't let others make you feel ashamed or some type of way for asking for help. If you ask for help and they turn around and ask about your husband or mate, just state that he's unavailable and you need help. The person is either going to help you or decline. I only ask for assistance from a person twice before I stop asking.

People who want to help you, will help you, without asking a lot of questions. You don't have to tell people a sob story or give an excuse for your mate (or lack thereof) or tell people all your business. People are going to help you or not, based only on the fact that you asked them. Simple as that. If they won't help you, someone else will. Find people who are willing *and* able to help. You'll be surprised where you can find help.

When you start asking for help you will see who is really in your tribe and who isn't. Don't assume your sister or mother or cousin or best friend or mother-in-law will make great tribe members. Tribe membership should not be based on blood or marriage. See who is a good fit based on personality, skills, willingness to help, and availability. Maybe some women are good in case of emergency only, which is fine.

In asking for help I realized that I wasn't getting what I needed simply because I hadn't asked. This might be happening to you. People may think you have it all together and admire your ability to have it all. Meanwhile you are suffering and miserable. When I started asking for help, the women in my tribe were compassionate and eager to assist. They didn't ask a million questions, and they offered future assistance. I came to learn who I could count on for what and asked for assistance when needed. Some women in my tribe also committed to regular assistance, which was a huge help.

When choosing your tribe recognize the difference between regular members and in case of emergency friends. Your regular members have a place, understand the boundaries, and adhere to the rules. In case of emergency members are good for simple favors or bail outs. Don't confuse the two. When you figure out which women you can count on, and under what circumstances, you'll be better for it.

You say, "Chris I don't trust easily." I hear you and I understand why you feel that way. I've had trust broken by women in my tribe. Some situations were able to be mended, such as differences of opinion or accidently hurting each others' feelings, but others weren't. When dealing with your tribe keep the human factor in mind and respect the skillset of each tribe member.

As you build your tribe you may find that some tribe members are only good for certain seasons in your life. If so, then let them go. Membership in your tribe shouldn't be like the mob. "You'll be tested to get in, and once you are out, you are dead to me." Don't be bitter. You'll know when it is time for someone to go.

Wish her well and move along. Forgive and most of all, drop the drama.

Recognize that each woman has skills as well as flaws. Tribes are great to have and like any other relationship, take work. It's worth it! Nothing is more amazing than women supporting women. Every time I have an event or receive an award, there is at least one woman from my tribe there with me. Your tribe is waiting for you, just take the steps!

Tips for Treasuring Your Tribe:
1. Seek out different types of women with different skillsets
2. Be selective in who joins your tribe
3. Select tribe members who are willing and able to help
4. Tribe membership is give and take

Chapter 6:
Ready, Set, GROW!

Let's Get Organized

"Ask and it will be given to you; seek and you will find; knock and the door will be opened to you." Matthew 7:7 (NIV)

I hope you are finding yourself longing for a new normal. Your life must become your life again and not just a resource for others. In order to make this life work, you must make your life work for YOU and YOUR needs.

As women we already stand on the ledge and before we know it, we've jumped clean off without a warning to others. Meanwhile you KNOW you've been there a while and didn't know what to do or how to say it. I found myself on a proverbial ledge one day with one foot over the side. I was doing too much in every area of my life and it was killing me. Like me, you've probably reached the near breaking point too and you've decided to do something to save yourself. So how do you save yourself? Organization will help to keep you from coming unglued.

Ready? Let's get organized. Make a list of ALL your commitments, including how often you do them, and what exactly you do. I mean every meeting, volunteer event, school, consulting work, boards you serve on, committees, miscellaneous obligations, things you help the kids with, things you help your mate with, things you help other people with, etc. This space may be a bit small, so I suggest using notebook paper or an Excel spreadsheet or an app on your phone or send an e-mail to yourself. Here's an outline you can use.

Organization	What I Do	When I do It
XYZ Board	Meetings	Monthly
	Data	As Needed
	Review doc	Quarterly

I did this exercise and when I saw the list, I instantly saw the problem. I was doing too much!!! You probably are too. No wonder you are stressed out and ready to quit. That's too much AND for one person and you may need to make some adjustments.

Prioritize your list to determine, what you really must do and what you can let go of or step away from. In prioritizing your list determine what YOU have to do yourself and what can be done by others. For example, what can your kids help with more and what can your mate do? If you don't have a mate, what can you get a family member or friend to do, or afford for a service to do?

When I was a single mother my brother would cut my grass in exchange for eating at my house. If family or friends aren't an option, look at other resources. When you see the flyers or door tags, start looking at them. Maybe there is something in there that can help you. Try locating services on Groupon or

Living Social. You'll want to look for options and opportunities.

If you have kids to care for, then get them organized too. They can help to make this life work as well. Create a schedule for them and stay on top of them to ensure they do what they are supposed to. Post it somewhere such as on the refrigerator so that they can clearly see it. Everyone age two or above can help. Yes, even the toddler has responsibility in my house. The kids must learn to be more self-sufficient. Everything can't be on you ALL the time.

Here are a few websites with articles and resources that may help:

https://workingparentresource.com/

https://www.webmd.com/parenting/features/chores-for-children#1

After thinking and being honest with yourself, you may realize that some commitments must go. I know I got rid of some things. Look at the benefit compared to the time and energy you invest. Continue doing the most important things, but you may want to scale back your efforts. You don't have to attend *every* event. Look at the calendar, select a few key events, determine when you'll volunteer, and that's it. No phone call or email should change that. Say "NO" and mean it.

With some commitments you might just need to make minor changes and you'll be good to go. In other instances, there won't be anything you can change, which is okay. Then there will be those things that cost more time and energy to do than the benefit they provide. Some of them may even cause you a lot of stress, so those things must go.

The things that you can step down from immediately, you should step down from. The things that you can't step down from without causing great pain or problems, you'll want to develop your exit plan. Give notice of your departure and a date. Get your paperwork and other affairs in order in preparation for your departure.

You say, "Chris, this all sounds great, but how do I do it? Getting organized is a challenge for me." Take it a little bit at a time. You don't have to do it all in one day, but don't procrastinate! Even a little each day is progress. Here's the plan.

Plan, Prep, Organize, GO!
1. Make the list of your obligations
2. Prioritize the list
    a. What must be done?
       i.   What must be done by you?
      ii.   What must be done, but can be done by others?
    b. What must be done, but less often?
    c. What should be done, but isn't critical?

3. Prioritize and eliminate the unnecessary
    a. What's critical and important?
    b. What's important, but not critical?
    c. What things would be nice to do, but aren't critical or important?
4. Transfer responsibility (where appropriate) with training and instructions
5. Do anything less often, that doesn't have to be done as often as you do it
6. Prepare for each week in advance
    a. Select clothing for the week
        i. Include one additional outfit option and include at least one outfit or accessory that makes you feel good about yourself
    b. Have the kids select their clothing for the week
    c. Determine the menu for each day
        i. Let each kid select a meal
        ii. Ask your mate to prepare at least one meal a week
    d. Determine the chores and to dos

e. Determine the amount of time devoted to each task in your day

7. Build a routine and follow it

a. Build in a day of rest or time for yourself

When you make your list of commitments take the time to think about the return on investment (ROI) for your commitments. Ask yourself these questions and take time to really think.

Why are you doing this?

_____

_____

What's the value of this to you or to your household?

_____

_____

Is this a burden or a benefit?

_____

_____

What will happen if "YOU" don't do this? What else does this impact?

_____

_____

Does this have to be done this way? How could this be done more effectively?

_____

_____

Ask, Believe, Plan, Pray, Obey, Receive

So, you've figured out the here and now, but how do you move forward? Growth includes preparing for the next level. Much like the 80/20 rule in finance, you must govern your life the same way. You should spend 80%

of your time on the life you have now and 20% on preparing for the life you want. If 20% isn't getting you where you want to go, then adjust, but don't neglect the life you have. I'm sure you noticed the bible verse that started this chapter, so I just wanted to let you know, the next section of this chapter is faith based.

Tap into your faith and let it be your guide. If you ask for it, believe it will happen, and obey God, then it will be so. God gives us the desires of our hearts and if we cry out to him, he will hear us and help us. Now, this isn't a one-time deal, because God isn't a genie in a bottle awaiting our calls. Go into relationship with God and let Him guide you. Seek Him and He will help you.

Let me put it another way. Write down the desires of your heart, believe it can happen, set a plan in motion, stay encouraged, stick to the plan (adjust where needed), and don't give up. Go after what you want with all your heart and might. If it is meant for you to have, then it will be yours. If after all your effort, you find that what you want is out of reach, then look at the timing of what you want and look at your circumstances.

Sometimes what you want is out of reach because it isn't the proper timing for where you are or need to be. Maybe it isn't no, but not yet. Maybe you aren't ready. The right thing in the wrong timing is a disaster! This I know all too well. The key is consistency and following the plan set out before you.

Ask, Believe, Plan, Pray, Obey, Receive
"Now him who is able to do immeasurably more than all we ask or imagine according to his power that is at work within us."
Ephesians 3:20 NIV

To **Ask** is to figure out what you need or want and to make your requests known to God and the universe. The thing with most people is they truly don't know what they want. You think you know, but when it comes down to it, you really don't. If you do already know, then please feel free to skip down to the next section. If you really don't know or if you feel you need to refine or redefine your thoughts, then keep reading. In order to get something better, you first must know what better looks like and what better is. It's like George Harrison wrote in the song *Any Road*, "And if you don't know where you're going...Any road will take you there."

Let's think about your (1) needs, (2) wants, and (3) desires. Then make a list for each section. Note, that they aren't one in the same. For instance, a reliable car is a need, and a brand-new car is a want, but a Lexus IS350 is a desire. Do you see the difference? Good, so let's start making that list. What are your actual needs? For example, maybe you need better housing or a reliable vehicle or better childcare or something else.

Take a moment to think about your needs, wants, and desires. You may have to start on this and revisit it as your thoughts become clear. Don't get stuck, just write and revise. Something great will come out.

What are your needs? What are the non-negotiable items that are severely impacting your quality of life? I mean what things that if you don't get them, will cause some serious consequences in your life? Those are your needs.

_____

_____

_____

_____

_____

_____

Now that you've gotten your list of needs together, what do you want? Identify the things that make you say, "If I had _____ my life would be better." For me it's uninterrupted, scheduled time alone to do something I like.

What are your wants? What would make your life easier or more bearable?

_____

_____

_____

_____

_____

_____

Once you have your wants together, what are your desires? Now this part you are allowed some creativity and dreaming. For me this includes a five-day vacation twice a year to spend time alone or with one person in my tribe who helps me to recharge. Some of your desires may be a bit lofty, but I know some parts of it are manageable.

What are your desires? This is your perfect world scenario. This is your, genie in a bottle list of unlimited wishes.

_____

_____

_____

_____

When you have your list of needs, wants, and desires, identify the top three for each section. You'll focus on your top three in the next few sections. The most significant part of the ask is knowing what you want. Be bold, be brave, and most of all, be better.

In selecting your top three, think about what's possible then **Believe** that what you need, want, and desire are possible. Believing doesn't mean being disillusioned or naive. To believe is to refocus your thoughts, energy and efforts on what's possible. If you believe you can do or be or have something, then you shall.

Believing is planting a seed in the mind and is critical in moving toward your goals. If you don't see it or believe that you can get it, then there is no point in ever thinking you'll get it. To put it another way, to believe is to think that something is possible, even when you don't know how it'll happen. For some, this is called having faith, and for others this is trusting that the universe will provide what you believe and move toward. Believe in yourself, your needs, your wants, your desires, then develop a plan.

They say faith without work is dead, and so too is a belief without a plan. To **Plan** is to find ways to accomplish your needs, wants, and desires. What can you do or change or stop doing that will help you to accomplish your top three? For instance, the plan for getting a reliable car could include checking your credit report and getting your credit in order. It could be seeing what you could redirect in your budget in order to save for a down payment. It could mean letting go of your current vehicle and carpooling or taking public transportation for a while or applying for a better job that pays more money. You get the picture.

In planning you must identify what YOU can do to move closer to what you need, want, and desire. When making your plan, you should have goals and tasks that you'll complete on your way to meeting each goal. Your goal setting process should be S.M.A.R.T.E.R:

1. **S**pecific
2. **M**easurable
3. **A**ttainable
4. **R**elevant
5. **T**ime-based
6. **E**valuated
7. **R**e-evaluated

www.smart-goals-guide.com

Know what you are doing and where you are going. Determine how you'll get there and the steps along the way. Note, once you have accomplished your top three needs, wants, and desires, revisit the list and see what's next. Revise and update the list as needed.

After you make your plan, let it sit for a day or two so that you can think it over better and make modifications. You plan then you **Pray** over the plan. A plan is great and will be even better when it is developed in conjunction with the Lord. In developing your plan, you may want to consult a trusted friend or family member who believes in your dreams. Put the plan into the atmosphere and see how it sounds.

Does your plan make sense?
A lot   Some   Not At All
Will your plan get you where you are trying to go?
A lot   Some   Not At All
Are you in line with what God is telling you to do?
A lot   Some   Not At All

For me, the most important and difficult part of this process is obedience. Once you have determined the plan and sought wise council, you then must **Obey** the direction you are being taken in. This is where your faith is tested. Your faith will need to grow as you work the plan. There will be some parts which are a bit muddy or that might not make sense at the time, but are meant to set things up for your good later.

Some say obedience is doing what you are told, when you are told, with a happy heart. I'm not always good at the "happy heart" part. Without the "happy heart" part you are essentially being partially obedient. Partial obedience is total disobedience so you can't kind of obey. You are either in or out. There is nothing in between! This may seem like a lot, but it's worth it. So, stay obedient even when things get rocky or unpredictable.

To **Receive** means to reap the benefits of your efforts. You have the vision, set some goals, made the plan, worked the plan, and now it's time to see the results. The funny thing about the receiving season is that it requires work too. You don't just sit back and wait for things to roll in. Receiving is much like harvesting.

In harvest season you gather the ripe crops, which are the rewards for your effort. However, it isn't as easy as just getting the crops. On a farm, the harvest season is a season of work because the crops don't just fall into your bag. You must work to retrieve them. Your character development is just as important, if not more, than the experience itself. When working to receive, you will be challenged to stretch and grow. This will strengthen you and prepare you for the next level.

Tips for Growth:
1. Ask, Believe, and Plan
2. Stick to the plan
3. Don't give up!
4. Challenge yourself to grow

The Wrap Up

You've done an amazing job at this point! You made the list, prioritized by importance, determined the responsible party, trained or provided instructions (with explanation), redetermined frequency of tasks, and stopped doing anything that wasn't producing fruit. You've also dealt with the here and now plus set some plans in motion for the future. You've set yourself up for growth.

If you have put in the work, the growth will happen along the way. The growth is found on the journey if you'll accept it. Things may be rough at times, but how much you grow is up to you. You can see challenges as stress or opportunities for growth. How much growing are YOU willing to do?

So, thank you for joining me on this journey. I hope that you made it through each chapter and collected the tools you needed. You answered the questions, and you have done the work. By now you should be on your way to transforming.

The work doesn't stop here. This is only the beginning. Where you go from here depends on how as far you are willing to grow. Self-reflection is key so do it and do it often. Transformation takes time. You shouldn't be who you were five years ago and five years from now you shouldn't be who you are today. Keep striving and transforming. You got this!

Once you've done the work to find yourself, don't be so quick to lose yourself in someone else. Remember, don't disconnect emotionally or leave physically. You truly must make a conscious decision, a covenant between you and the universe that no matter what, you're making this life work so you can live your best life.

About The Author

Dr. Chris Hubbard Jackson is an author, speaker, researcher, woman, daughter, wife, and mother. In becoming fed up with the AND in her life, she decided to take control and use writing as a release. In writing she found joy, a safe place for her sense of humor, and practical tips to refocus her life.

Dr. Chris describes her life as a bit of a zigzag road mixed with lightning bolts, lots of curves, and sharp turns. It's had just enough challenges to make her light up but not quite enough to make her smoke.

She has a passion for empowering women to live their best life by eliminating the unnecessary commitments in their lives. Often referred to as the "go to friend," Dr. Chris uses her love for God, life experiences, along with her background in education and psychology to deliver colorful yet classy advice with a bit of flair.